W9-AWO-834

What's a BIRD?
¿Qué es un AVE?

Anna Kaspar

Traducción al español:
Eduardo Alamán

PowerKiDS
press.

New York

Published in 2013 by The Rosen Publishing Group, Inc.
29 East 21st Street, New York, NY 10010

First Edition

Editor: Amelie von Zumbusch   Traducción al español: Eduardo Alamán
Book Design: Ashley Drago

Photo Credits: Cover, p. 5 Hemera/Thinkstock; pp. 6, 10, 18 iStockphoto/Thinkstock; p. 9 © www.iStockphoto.com/Richard Goerg; pp. 13, 14 Shutterstock.com; p. 17 © www.iStockphoto.com/Pauline S. Mills; p. 21 © www.iStockphoto.com/Frank Leung; p. 22 Jupiterimages/Photos.com/Thinkstock.

Library of Congress Cataloging-in-Publication Data

Kaspar, Anna.
 [What's a bird. Spanish & English]
 What's a bird? = ¿Qué es un ave? / by Anna Kaspar. — 1st ed.
     p. cm. — (All about animals = Todo sobre los animales)
 Includes index.
 ISBN 978-1-4488-6702-8 (library binding)
 1. Birds—Juvenile literature. I. Title. II. Title: ¿Qué es un ave?
 QL676.2.K3718 2013
 598—dc23
                                        2011024119

Web Sites: Due to the changing nature of Internet links, PowerKids Press has developed an online list of Web sites related to the subject of this book. This site is updated regularly. Please use this link to access the list:
www.powerkidslinks.com/aaa/bird/

3 1907 00314 5496

Manufactured in the United States of America

CPSIA Compliance Information: Batch #CS12PK: For Further Information contact Rosen Publishing, New York, New York at 1-800-237-9932

Contents / Contenido

Birds are animals with **feathers**. How many birds can you name?

_____

Las aves son animales con **plumas**. ¿Cuántas aves conoces?

All birds have **beaks**.
Australian pelicans have the
longest beaks.

Todas las aves tienen **picos**.
Los pelícanos australianos
tienen los picos más largos.

Birds have **wings**. Most birds use their wings to fly.

Las aves tienen **alas**. La mayoría de las aves usan las alas para volar.

Not all birds fly. Penguins use their wings to swim.

No todas las aves vuelan. Los pingüinos usan sus alas para nadar.

Mother birds lay **eggs**. Baby birds break out of the eggs.

Las aves mamá ponen **huevos**. Las aves bebé salen de los huevos.

Birds care for their babies. Many birds bring food to their babies.

Las aves cuidan a sus bebés. Muchas aves llevan comida a sus bebés.

Some birds fly to warmer places for the winter. Arctic terns make the longest yearly trip.

Muchas aves vuelan a lugares cálidos durante el invierno. El gaviotín ártico es el ave que vuela más lejos cada año.

Different kinds of birds eat different foods. Woodpeckers eat mostly bugs.

No todas las aves comen lo mismo. Los pájaros carpinteros comen, principalmente, bichos.

19

Bald eagles are the national bird of the United States. Fish is their main food.

El águila calva es el ave nacional de los Estados Unidos. El águila calva come mucho pescado.

Some birds are known for their songs. African gray parrots can learn to say words!

Algunas aves son conocidas por su canto. ¡El loro gris africano puede aprender algunas palabras!

WORDS TO KNOW/
PALABRAS QUE DEBES SABER

beak/
(el) pico

eggs/
(los) huevos

feathers/
(las) plumas

wing/
(las) alas

INDEX

F
food(s), 15,
19–20

U
United
States, 20

S
songs, 23

W
wings, 8, 11

ÍNDICE

A
alas, 8, 11

C
canto, 23

comida(s),
15, 19–20

E
Estados
Unidos, 20